CALL ME WHEN YOU'RE FREE

CALL ME WHEN YOU'RE FREE

A Collection of Poetry
and Spoken Word

PJ

PHOENIX JAMES

CALL ME WHEN YOU'RE FREE

Copyright © 2022 Prince-James Harrison.

For any questions about usage, please email contact@PhoenixJamesOfficial.com

First Edition: 2022

ISBN: 978-1-7397925-8-9 (Paperback)
ISBN: 978-1-7397925-9-6 (Ebook)

Cover Artwork & Design by Phoenix James.
Book Design & Formatting by Phoenix James.

Visit the author's website at www.PhoenixJamesOfficial.com or email him at phoenix@PhoenixJamesOfficial.com

DEDICATION

To all who find answers
To the many questions
They didn't know they had
To all who never noticed
The cold and the darkness
Until feeling warmth from the fire
And seeing its light flickering in

And to a young boy
Many moons ago
Who would let his mind wander
And his imagination run free
Exploring worlds within a world
And ideas not yet encountered

Thank you for your inquisitiveness
Your burning desire to understand
To make sense of all and everything
To uncover, to discover and to learn
I am who I am today because of you

I hope you find this a satisfactory effort
And that it doesn't disappoint you
I hope you're impressed and overjoyed.

CONTENTS

ALL OF THESE PLACES 1
ALMOST DROWNED 3
ANKLE BRACELET APPEAL 5
CARDS ON THE TABLE 15
CURIOUS ABOUT VIDEO 24
DEVELOPMENT & PATIENCE 26
ENERGY DRAINERS 30
LIMP HANDSHAKES 34
MAN RAPED BY WOMAN 36
MASS APPEAL 38
MIGHT BE A LESBIAN 52
MISSING SUMMER 70
ON LOVE & MARRIAGE 72
ON TINDER 82
PATIENCE OVERALL 85
PRESERVATION OF THE PRICELESS 90
RISE OF THE ROBOTS 97
SELF REFLECTIONS 106
SOCIALLY AWKWARD 113
STEAMY SEX SCENE 122
TEACHER ATTRACTION 127
THE KILL OF CHASING 138
TRUTH IS OUT THERE 146
WAY OF THE WORLD 159
WHAT I LIKE IN BED 168
YOU ARE ENOUGH 171
YOUR AUTHOR 172

ALL OF THESE PLACES

I'm in the park again
A different park this time
I've actually decided
I've got a list
I'm going to go through
Of London parks
And I'm going to
Check them out
All of them
That I haven't visited
Kensington
And Greenwich
Are two that are
On the top
Of my list for sure
Just because I've heard
Good things about them
I've been here my whole life
Well most of it
And I haven't seen
All of these places
I think it's terrible
People come
From other countries

Specifically
With these places
On their little map
To go to
That they're not
Going to leave
Before they go
To visit these places
And we have them right here
And we don't go to them
It's just funny to me
And sad
And out of order.

ALMOST DROWNED

I went on a school trip
To Wales
When I was about ten
I got into the swimming pool
I ended up in the deep end
I couldn't swim
I started drowning
I went down twice
I went down the third time
They say you go up
And down
Three times
Before you drown
The last time I went down
A man pulled me up
At that moment
I was scratching at his legs
Drowning basically
I guess he realised
At that point
That I might be drowning
It was a while though
Before he actually reacted
And pulled me out

I feel if not for that
I might not be here
Right now
I always remember that
I think I've always
Had a little fear
Of the water
Since that time
I was ten years old
I never forget that
Wales school trip
Nearly died at ten
I'm glad I didn't
Nearly was a goner
I stopped
Going in the water
As much
I definitely had a fear of it
I've been
In a lot deeper water since
Both literally
And figuratively.

ANKLE BRACELET APPEAL

I feel as if
All the ills
And evils
Of this world
Could be easily
Corrected
Could be easily
Put right
Could be easily
Remedied
If more women
Wore ankle bracelets
I do
I just feel
That's what's wrong
With society
I just feel
That's the problem
It's the answer
To everything
That is wrong
On this planet
With this world
With its people

With human beings
All the negative
That we see
It's just down to that for me
I think more women
Need to wear
Ankle bracelets
Like the old days
Bring the importance
Back to them
Like you have
At an Indian wedding
For example
Or you know
The Egyptians
Ankle bracelets
Were a big thing
Still are
Just not enough
I feel
The world of women
Need to embrace
Ankle bracelets
Anklets
I'm not talking about
Ankle chains

You know like
When someone's imprisoned
I don't mean shackles
I'm talking about jewellery
Ankle bracelets
Charms
That kind of thing
The little ones that jingle
Little pretty charms on them
Jingle jingle
That's what I'm talking about
Gold
Silver
You know
Ankle bracelets
Anklets
I feel life will be better
I feel everybody will be happier
I feel life will be a more
Pleasant experience
If ankle bracelets are embraced
And adorned
On a regular basis
On a bigger level
Globally
We will heal a lot of the ills

Of our society
Of our communities
Of our planet
Ankle bracelets
Are a good thing
People take it lightly
They don't understand
That this
Is where change
Will come about
When women
Start adorning
Ankle bracelets
Like you have Summer
Coming up now
And if a few women
Put on a couple
Of ankle bracelets
No one's going to be upset
About anything
Guaranteed
Try it
If you're a woman
Put on an ankle bracelet
This summer
And see

How the world changes
If you're a man
Encourage other women
To wear ankle bracelets
And see how the world changes
Call this
A public service announcement
Call this a request
Call this what you want
But know the truth is
Ankle bracelets
Will be the remedy
To what I call
The ills of our society
The evils
The negative
All the bad things
About this world
Will turn on its head
I guarantee you
What it would need
Is enough people
To embrace this
And take it seriously
And this summer
Wear more ankle bracelets

It's just necessary
I love ankle bracelets
I think they're a thing of beauty
I think they are necessary
I think they should be worn more
Made more visible
I know what I'm talking about
We are in May now
Summer is approaching
Summer is almost upon us
There is no reason why
Any woman
Should not be adorning
An ankle bracelet
With her attire this summer
And every summer to follow
And those of you who are
I must speak about those of you
Who are already doing this
Because I would be remiss
If I didn't
I applaud you
I thank you
I respect you
And I am always
Happy to see you

For everyone else
Please take heed
The world needs more
Ankle bracelets
If you wear ankle bracelets
Or an ankle bracelet
Let me know
I want to see
How many people
Still do the right thing
Let me know
I mean it's pretty hard
To be upset
I'm talking from
Personal experiences
It's pretty hard
To be upset
When you see a woman
Wearing an ankle bracelet
It brightens my day
And I know I'm not alone
And this is why
I speak on how I feel
I feel that the world
With more women
Wearing ankle bracelets

Will be a better place
Sincerely
So let's do it
Summer is approaching
You have plenty of time
Let's get them on
And out there
You know it's right
You know
It's right
You know that saying
It's the little things
The little things
It's the little things
Ankle bracelets
More ankle bracelets
This summer
Wow
There's going to be
Some happy people
Walking around
It's true
It's just true
People are going to be happier
Because women
Are walking around

Wearing ankle bracelets
More than usual
This is my hope
That people
Will take this information
And acknowledge this truth
That they may have overlooked
And adopt
An ankle bracelet
If they haven't already
And continue to do so
If they already do so
And see
How the world will change
The world
Is not a great place
In a lot of ways
You know
There's a lot of bad things
Happening in the world
That could be bettered
That could be alleviated
That could be stopped
Basically
It's the little things
That are going to do that

They are going to go a long way
Towards that change
Towards that betterment
Ankle bracelets.

CARDS ON THE TABLE

A lot of times
People are just
Following the crowd
They don't really
Have any thoughts
Of their own on things
And if everyone
Is doing this whole thing
Of not coming forward
And speaking up
And letting the man
Have his role
Then everyone is
Doing the same thing
And no one's
Getting anywherc
Because everyone is
Doing this defensive thing
Against guys
Rather than
Coming forward
And letting themselves
Be vulnerable
I think we all have it

I think there's always
That vulnerability there
The woman
Doesn't want to say
What she thinks
What her idea is
Or give up her opinion
Her thoughts
How she feels
Before the guy does
She may be waiting
To say I love you forever
But she's not going to
Say anything
Until he says it
That kind of thing
Or not to say how she feels
Or express herself
Or even offer
An idea on something
Wants the guy
To make the call
To say what it is
Like what do you think
Do you like me
What do you think

All this kind of stuff
Not yes I like you
That kind of stuff
It's a little bit cat and mouse
It's a cat and mouse thing
It's not giving the full thing
It's like maybe
Or what do you think
Always avoiding making a decision
Avoiding giving up their position
Where they're at
Avoiding showing their cards
Avoiding showing their hand
They're avoiding
Being in the vulnerable position
That's what I mean
It's this cat and mouse thing
Like this chase thing
Guys trying to get to that place
But the woman
Is not allowing herself
To be vulnerable in that way
Showing her hand
How she feels
What her thoughts are
On the subject

She wants to
Hear his thoughts first
The question
Is said by the guy
What do you think
Of blah blah blah
And the woman
Because she doesn't want
To show her hand
She's like, I don't know
What do you think
It's always that kind of chase
You know
That cat and mouse
Having your cards hidden away
Holding your cards
Close to your chest type thing
It's very much a thing
It's common
It's something that women do
I'm not saying
That men don't do it
And there are other dynamics
Obviously
To be talked about
And discussed

That are involved
In the whole thing
But I'm just focusing now
As a heterosexual male
On how I've experienced it
With women
It's a thing that happens
That I've experienced a lot
Because they don't want to
Show that vulnerability
So if I if I'm to meet
A woman who
Doesn't conduct herself
In that way
Or she doesn't act that way
It's refreshing
Because it's not the norm
It's not the normal thing
The norm is
To have this whole
Not showing the cards
Not laying out
Everything on the table
Sometimes
It can come across defensive
Holding back

Not giving out their feeling
Of what they're really feeling
Before they know how you feel
Sometimes
They might not
Answer the question
Of how they feel
They will avoid the answering
And would get your answer
And still not tell you their side
So then they've got a point
It's like a game
They've scored a point
Because they haven't said
How they feel
But they found out
How you feel
So it's like a game
It's this whole
Cat and mouse thing
It's very common
I've experienced that more
Than I have experienced
A woman
Who comes out and says
I feel this way

About this thing
Or to be the first one to say
Or express the emotion
Of her feelings
About me
Or a situation
That's been more common
To me
Than a woman
Who has come out
And said it
And showed her cards
And put her cards on the table
Will be the first one
To say I love you
And all this kind of stuff
Like does it even matter
Who says it first
I can see why they may want
To not say I love you first
That's a difficult one
I get that
That's another thing
That could be talked out
A bit more
But that's just

A rough example
Of having cards to the chest
And not wanting to show them
Love might have been
A bit extreme
Because that's a whole
Other conversation
But you know what I mean
Just ideas about things
And opinions about things
It may be as simple as
Coming out of the cinema
You may go to see a movie
You come out
To these little things
That are really unnecessary
But I get it
I do get why it happens
But you know
You come out of the movie
And the guy says
What do you think of the film
What do you think
And rather than give
Their expression
Or explanation

Or opinion
Of what they thought
Of the film
They'll redirect
The question
Back to you
They will kind of
Skirt around it
Then they'll ask
What do you think
That kind of thing
This is a rough example
I don't know
If it's a very good example
But that's definitely
One of them
Not showing their cards
They want to know
What you think first
Before they say anything
Before they show their hand.

CURIOUS ABOUT VIDEO

The game has changed
I was trying
To get back up
On video again
Could you imagine
If I carried on
Doing video
And vlogging
From 2009
Until now
Recording
And documenting
Everything
Every moment
Pretty much
Documenting my day
Like I was doing
Back then
But I just
Didn't keep it up
I so wish I did
Imagine if
You were one of
The early people

Who ever started
Uploading stuff
Imagine where you'd be now
If you didn't stop doing it
Anyone now
If they put their energy
Into building that
I mean
You've got be good
Obviously
But totally
With commitment
Consistency
Dedication
And persistence
I think the same
Or similar results
Could definitely
Be achieved for sure
And not just
With video
But with anything.

DEVELOPMENT & PATIENCE

All is well
l can't complain
I've been really enjoying
This weather of late
It's been great
It seems it's been
The longest summer
We've had in a while
And I'm thankful
That this is the year
I've chosen
To embrace summer
And sunshine
Differently
From I have in recent years
Missing the whole thing
Because it's like
You get two weeks of summer
If you're underground
For two weeks
You've missed summer right
All is well
Just working on my stuff
Keeping out of trouble

Creating
And more creating
And it's been amazing
I've been traveling
For some time
And that's been
Really good for me
In terms of having time
To just be outside
Of the working environment
You get to look at
Where you are
And for me it's been good
Because I've got to see
Where I'm at
And where I want to be
And are they the same
Am I going the right way
For that to happen
For me
To get from where I am now
To where I want to go
So it's been good
I've been in a good place
Because I have found
More direction

With things I'm doing
And wanting to do
So all is good
It's been a good couple of years
It changes
You know
What you wanted to do
At sixteen
Can change
When you get to twenty
And so on it goes
Until you
Find where you're happy
Where you're comfortable
It's just
We don't at the time
Know that all it needs
Is patience
And it's okay to not know
And to change our minds
I wish someone
Would have
Taught me patience
In school
I wish it was
Part of the curriculum

Patience
Patience and kindness
All those things
That you don't get taught
NLP
Personal development
And stuff like that
As a subject
I think that should be taught
In school
Neurolinguistic programming
It should be on the curriculum.

ENERGY DRAINERS

My friends
Please get
The energy drainers
Energy siphoners
People that are just around
To siphon your energy
Drain your energy
Take your energy
Steal your energy
And they're not
Having anything
To offer in return
Not able to refill the cup
Please get them
Out of your life
As quickly
And swiftly
As possible
By any means necessary
Of course
Don't kill anybody
Don't go to jail
But use necessary measures
To remove these people

From your domain
From your person
From your space
As quickly
And swiftly
As possible
These people
Have no intention
Of filling you back up
When they come around you
And drain your energy
They are thieves
They are stealers
They are robbers
And they have
Nothing to give you
Know who they are
I'm telling you this
Because you know
Who they are
Please get them
Out of your life
Get them away from you
Don't contemplate anything
Don't contemplate
What they have to offer

Because
If they haven't offered it yet
At this stage
They will not
Be offering anything
They will just
Drain your energy
And they will just take
And take
And continue to take
And the more you give
The more
They will continue to take
Get these energy drainers
Out of your life
As quickly
And swiftly
As possible
For your benefit
Energy drainers
They exist
They walk among us
Around you
You know who they are
They want your energy
They want your time

Because
If they have your time
They are in your space
Having that time
They'll also get your energy
They know that
And you know that
Those people
Who are upset
When you're unable
To give them
That time and energy
Those people
Who have nothing
To offer in return
Those people
You know them by name
I don't know who they are
I know for me
I don't know for you
But you do
Please get them
Out of your life
Please help yourself
And remove them
Out of your life.

LIMP HANDSHAKES

It's the worst
It's one thing
That I don't like
It's the worst
We'll have to do one
To show each other
What we're talking about
It's cringy
I question that person
What they're about
Could be shaking
A pedophiles hand
Handshakes like that
You get what I mean
That limp
Non hand
It's not even
A handshake
It's nothing
So pointless
You know
This is probably a bit different
But you know
What it's also like

You know when guys
Do that air hug thing
Have you seen that
When they greet each other
There's no hug
There's no handshake
I don't actually
Know what they're doing
They just kind of
Lean in
And lean out
You know
What I'm talking about
They lean in
And lean out
A guy did that to me
He's a security guard
He went to do that to me
I said no
Let's hug properly
Or let's do nothing.

MAN RAPED BY WOMAN

Yes
One hundred percent
This could be
A group of women
It could be one woman
Who is just stronger
Than that man
Totally
I mean
It happened to me
I've been raped
By a woman before
No I'm joking
It was all consensual
But you're right
I could be
I could have been
You know
Anyone
Any man could be
Overpowered
By a woman
And taken advantage of
Sexually

It's very true
We see it
There's a lot
Of things going on
Why people behave
The way they behave
Because some of these things
Have happened to them
And they haven't been able
To speak about it.

MASS APPEAL

You say
People say to you
Why don't you lie
About your age
So are these people
That lie about their own age
Obviously they are
If they're encouraging
You to do it
I imagine
I mean
You wouldn't do it
Unless you actually
Do it yourself
I'm assuming
Why would you say
To someone
Why don't you
Lie about your age
If they don't do it themselves
I'm assuming
These are all women
That do that
Men lie too of course

But don't you find
It's more of a woman thing
I can see men
Lying about their age
Maybe
But I mean
What's the ratio
You know what I think
When women lie
About their age
I believe it's
Not with the intention
Of continuing
The lie forever
For the rest of their lives
Until they die
Carrying it to the grave
I believe
It's more so
To attract
The thing
Or the person to them
At that time
That they will receive
The benefit of that thing
At that time

And then later
They can reveal their age
Or like dating for example
I think lying about their age
Is more like bait
When you're fishing
You put the bait on the hook
And you catch the fish
And that's that
You've got it now
I don't think
They plan to lie about it
Until they carry it to the grave
I think it's just
To not scare people off
Especially in dating
And courting
And relationships and stuff
I think it's definitely
A baiting thing
Not to scare the person off
But to catch them
Then when they get into it
And they like each other
Then they will say
Do you know

How old I really am
I don't know
I could be wrong about that
I think it's more
That when the person
Is hooked in
And they kind of feel
They've got them
Then they will tell
Their real age
And they'll get on
With their lives
I think
They don't want to
Scare a potential mate off
By telling their real age
I think it's more that
It's funny
I think it can be more
Offensive
A man doing it
Because it's seen
That he has
No real need
I think women
Can kind of

Get away with it
Because it's so common
It's been done for so long
Women and their age thing
That clock ticking
Type of thing
The biological clock
Women are kind of excused
For their reasons
They're worried about
Their looks
And ageing
But I think
When a man does it
And he's found out
I think it's a worse thing
I think a worse punishment
Is justified
I can imagine
A young guy doing that
But not a guy past thirty-five
I don't think so
I don't see
A guy past thirty-five
Or thirty even
Lying about his age

Saying he's older
Unless there was
Some form
He was filling out
And it was going to
Benefit him in some way
To say he was older
I could see younger guys
Lying about their age
That kind of puts them
In favour with older women
I could see that
So that the woman
Is not thinking
Oh he's too young
It kind of puts him
In the bracket
That she would
Probably be going for
If he said his real age
Maybe she'd say
You're too young for me
I could see that
But that's got to be
Twenty-five
Nothing above that

Nothing above thirty for sure
I don't think so
I think any guy that's thirty
Is not going to be lying
About his age
To make himself older
Unless the woman
Has something against
The age thirty
She thinks it's too young
Or something like that
Or she says that
Then he might try
And notch his age up a bit
But I definitely think
That's an under thirties thing
Maybe even under twenty-fives
I mean come on
Do you see a guy
Thirty-five
Lying about his age
Making himself older
For what reason
Unless he's like I said
Filling out a form
Going for a job

Some opportunity
That he's required
To be older for
I could only see it then
But not to a woman
No way
It's just unthinkable
To be honest
I never did it anyway
But if I was going to do it
It would it be
When I was younger
If I was pursuing
An older woman
And I knew
That she would say
My age was too young
Then I might have done that
I could see why guys did it
I've never done that
I never had to
But I could see why
Because women are saying
No you're too young for me
You're just a boy
Then they wouldn't

Get the opportunity
But if they lie
And say they're a bit older
They may get in there
I could see that
But that's got to be
Under thirty
I don't know
What type of guys
You're talking to
As a forty year old woman
That they're having to lie
About their age to you
That's just funny
You've actually gone very quiet
I'm actually worried
You're talking about
Your own situation here
You could tell me
I'm not surprised
That you get lots of young guys
Approaching you
Lying about their age
So they can get with you
In a different circumstance
I might have

Done the same thing
Fortunately
I've never had to do that
Yeah I could see that
It's no shame in that
Young guys on your case
It's great
Are we on the same page
Are we talking
About the same thing
Okay
There's nothing wrong
With that at all
That's great
If young guys
Are looking at you
And thinking they want some
That's great
You say you find
Fifty and sixty insulting
And early twenties
To mid twenties
You find insulting as well
This is interesting
So it's not an age thing then
You're talking about

The person
And how they
Carry themselves
Okay I see
Because I was going to say
If that's your scale
You're getting guys
From early twenties
To mid twenties
Approaching you
And then you're getting guys
Age fifty to sixty
Approaching you
That's nothing to be mad at
That's saying to you
That you appeal
To a wide range
You appeal
To not just one small area
In terms of men's ages
You have mass appeal
I understand
That you're not for it
But what I would say
Is that just says
You have mass appeal

And that's something
To be very happy about
To be honest with you
What that's basically saying
Is that you have mass appeal
From age twenty to twenty-five
Then up to sixty
So you could go right up
Because that's going to be
Everything in between as well
Definitely
You're cool with those in between
But they don't approach you
I understand
Well that's still good though
That you've got young guys
Approaching you
And you've got older men
Approaching you too
That still says
You have mass appeal
Because I'm not
Either of those
I'm in between
And I find you very sexy
So I'll stand up

For the middle part
And that gives you
Mass appeal
I stand by that
It's true
You may not like the guys
That are approaching you
But that still says
That you have it
And you should be very
Happy about that
People are interested
In a wide range of ages
Do I get approached by women
Yes I do
Not so much
On the younger side though
I don't find
Maybe I'm naive
But I don't find it to be so
I find in my experience
More tend to be older
My age and older
It's fewer of the younger age
That I find approach me
Or show interested in me

In that way
I find it's older women
And women around my age
Going closer to mid thirties
Early thirties and down
I find not so much
Again maybe I'm just naive to it
I don't know
Maybe it's because
The older ones
Are more forthcoming
Is that the right expression
They are more forward
You know
Maybe
Who knows
I just know it's amazing
That you've got such mass appeal
I said it
And I stand by it
That's all that proves
It's true.

MIGHT BE A LESBIAN

You know
There's something I wonder
This is something that
Only occurred to me
As a heterosexual man
I'd say in the past few years
I mean
I've always known it
It's always been apparent
In the back of my mind
Somewhere
But it's like it dawned on me
All of a sudden
Within the past
Three years maybe
That not all women
Are heterosexual
Let me explain
Basically
You're out
You're on the street
You're in public
You see a woman
And naturally

She's good-looking
Attractive
You know
It just may be
A social gathering
Maybe a meeting
Maybe a chance encounter
On public transport
You make eye contact
Whatever
Or you're somewhere
And there's just
A woman about
Or women
And you forget
That not all women
Are heterosexual
Not all of those women
Are into guys
Not all of those women
Go for men
You forget
Happened to me
I wonder how many
Guys out there
Forget

When they're
Approaching women
Getting rejected by women
Getting blank stares
And dismissals from women
Whether they realise
That she's not
Being a certain way
Because it's about you
Or doesn't like you
She's just not into men
So she's not wasting her time
She's not wasting yours
She's just not giving you
Any energy
Any attention
She's just not even
Thinking that way
Because she's not into men
She is into women
So what you would normally get
From a heterosexual woman
Who is interested in men
May be slightly different
From what you get
From a woman

Who is not heterosexual
And not interested in men
Whatsoever
She's just not
Thinking of you in that way
She may smile at you
She may even say hello
But she's not thinking of you
In that way
Because she doesn't
Go for men
She's not attracted to men
She's a lesbian
I do wonder
How many other men
Have this
Awareness about them
When they're out
In the company of women
That they don't know
I do often consider this
A lot more now
When I'm in the company
Of a woman
That I don't know
Her sexual orientation

What she's into
She may be attractive
I'm single
I'm wondering
Is she single
She may well be single
But she may well not be
Into men whatsoever
So I'd be wasting my time
Pursuing that avenue
Going down that road
Making advances towards her
In that way
That's what I'm saying
And I wonder
How many other men
Have this
Consciousness about them
When approaching
Women on the street
At social events
At gatherings
Wherever it may be
That he happens to
Bump into a woman
Or cross paths with a woman

On a train platform
On a bus
At a party you know
In a shop
At a friend's house
It never used to occur to me
That she may be gay
Lesbian
Not into men
You know
It just
Never occurred to me
Until the past three years
It became more apparent
In my mind
When I'm in those
Situations
It just never
Crossed my mind
I think I would have taken
A lot more things
Less personal
Back in the day
If I had taken that
Into account more
Or if my

Awareness of it
Was more at that time
As it is now
Because we're just not
Living in that type of world
Where all women
Are heterosexual
And into men strictly
That's what it is
We live in it
That's it
There's other things going on
Besides my heterosexuality
That's basically
What I'm saying
Guys, tell me
When you are out
As a single man
Are you out
With this awareness
When you see a group
Of women
Are you aware
That there's a possibility
That none of that group
Of seven women

Hanging out together
A possibility
That they are not straight
That they could be all gay
They could be all lesbians
On a night out together
Doing their
Girly lesbian thing
And not looking
In your direction
In that way
Whatsoever
Couldn't care less
Whether you're single
Or not
They couldn't care less
Whether you're single
Gay
Straight
Or dead
Have you ever
Thought about that
I'm just curious
Is it just me
And my weird mind
I'm sure it's not

But I would love to hear
From the guys
Are you aware
What's your awareness like
Because I've only
Come into this thing
Recently
In the past few years
This understanding
Maybe longer
But I'd say
The past three years
The realisation
That not all women
Are looking in my direction
As single women
They're looking
At my girlfriend
You know
But definitely
Not looking at me
Looking at everyone else
Around me
That's female
Except me
In fact

Looks right through me
Like I'm not there
Not on purpose
Just because
It's not
What they're looking for
So you know
When you're not
Looking for something
You see everything else
You see what you're
Looking for
You're looking
In the direction
Of what you're looking for
You're not seeing
The thing
You're not looking for
Until you're looking for it
So yeah
I'd be curious to know
How many of the guys
Walk around
With this awareness
When they're out
Ready to go

And seek out the ladies
I mean
I wonder how many of them
See women
And think they're straight
They're into guys
Let me see if I can
You know
Get in there
Not realising
That hold on
I've forgotten something
She might not be into men
She may be a lesbian
I know I'm not the only one
I'm just very curious to know
And women
On that same subject
When you go out
And you spot a guy
And you're single
And you're ready to mingle
Do you ever consider
In that whole process
Going up the escalator
He's going one way

You're going the other
You make eyes
Do you ever consider
That he may be gay
Is that like a thing
That's in your head
Or not
Or you just
Don't think about that
Because I didn't
For a long time
I never thought
Hold on
These women
Are not paying me
Any attention
They're not even looking
In my direction
They're not even
Glancing this way
Am I invisible
No you're just a man
I'm not interested in men
That's probably what it was
I think now
Didn't used to think that

I find it very interesting
Came to mind
I'm curious
I want to know
Who goes out
As a single person
And has that in mind
When they're considering
Approaching
Eyeing up
Making eye contact with
Thinking about a person
That they've had their eye on
Does it cross their mind
In that whole initial process
That they may not be into you
Because of your gender
Interesting right
It's just one of those things
I never thought of
My awareness in that arena
Is a lot greater now
I'm just a lot more aware
In those situations
That I just may not be talking
To a straight

64

Heterosexual
Into men
Likes guys
Thinks guys are hot
Type of woman
It just never
Crossed my mind before
Just always thought
All women are straight
They're all into me
They all want me
Men, how many of you
Have overlooked this
When you're at a club
And you see
A group of women
Dancing around their handbags
Did it ever cross your mind
That not one of them
Might be into men
Not one
They may all be
A group of lesbians
Just out at a club
Enjoying themselves
And actually

They're looking
At the same women
You're looking at
Across the room
Has that ever
Crossed your mind
Let me know
I am curious
At your workplace
There's this new girl
Just started
You like her
You really like her
She looks nice
Has it ever
Crossed your mind
In that type of situation
That she may not even
Be into men
I mean
Clearly
If there's been
Nothing that's happened
That has indicated to you
That fact
Have you ever

Just thought
There's that possibility
What's probably
On your mind instead
Is has she got a boyfriend
I'd guess that's your question
If I think back
To how I used to think
It was only
Has she got a boyfriend
But not
Has she got a girlfriend
Not is she into women
There's a thing
Next time you're out
And you see a woman
This is for the men now
And the ladies too actually
Next time you're out
Single people
Next time you're out
And you see someone
That you find attractive
You know
Looks all right
Looks nice

I'm single
Maybe they're single
Let me know
If you consider
That they
May not even be straight
The opposite sex I mean
I'd be very interested
To know
Call it a
Public service announcement
To say
Be aware
That when you
See someone
You're attracted to
Of the opposite sex
They may not be interested
Because they're not into
The opposite sex
Not because
They think you're ugly
Or they're not
Interested in you
Or think you're
Not worth their time

68

Or you're below them
None of that
They just don't
See you in that way
Because you're
Not the sex
They go for.

MISSING SUMMER

Again
One of the things
I've really said
I'm going to do
This summer
Is spend a lot more time
Around nature
I've been getting out
To parks and stuff
Hanging out
It's absolutely amazing
It's the first year
I've said
I'm going to get out more
And spend time in nature
And enjoy the sun
Other than being
Locked away
In some dungeon
In the dark
No windows
Working away
Missing
The whole of summer

And then come out
And it's all winter again
I've done that
For many years
And I said
This year
I'm not
So I've been out more
Than I've been in
This whole time
One day
Twenty-four hours
That's it
Twelve hours of summer
Last year
That's what we had
That's why I missed it
I was probably asleep
In the dark somewhere
Probably slept through it
Just asleep
You know
An afternoon nap
I missed it.

ON LOVE AND MARRIAGE

When you don't
Want to leave
When that person
Will do things
That will make you
Very angry
They'll make you upset
They'll make you want to
Pull your hair out
Pull their hair out
Kill them
Bury them
Under the cellar
Bury them in the garden
But you won't want to leave
They'll make you scream
They'll make you shout
They'll make you cry
Because you love them
That much
But you won't want to leave
You won't want to
Be without them
You can't imagine life

Without them
You want to stay
In their presence
All the time
No matter how upset
They make you
No matter how angry
They make you
You don't even
Think about leaving
You don't think about
Not being in their presence
That's what I think love is
I think love is
Always wanting that person
To be around
Accepting that person
For who they are
Really
You know
Not trying to change them
Oh you know
They'll change
They'll change
I hope they change
Because I like them otherwise

Not wanting to change them
Liking them
Just the way they are
Accepting them
Even if
You don't like everything
That they are
You accept it
Because you love them
But coming back
To what I think
Most of all
Is nothing could happen
That would make you
Want to leave
They could do
The worst things
That's love to me
Some people
Could look at it
A different way
Some people
Could define it
A different way
Say there's different reasons
Why you might not

Want to leave
Whatever
But I think love is
When you can't
Imagine yourself
Without that person
You can't imagine
Your life
Without that person
No matter
What negatives happen
Or come from things
They may do
Or say
That's love
Even if
You do leave that person
You realise
You can't live without them
So you go back
And it stays like that
Because of the love
Whatever that connection is
Even if you do leave them
You realise
There's something

Missing in your life
And you have to
Be with them
Aside from violence
Aside from spousal abuse
I think if you're
Getting beaten up
By your partner
I think you definitely
Should leave
I make it clear
It doesn't include
Being beaten
By your partner
If your partner is beating you
You leave
You leave
And don't consider it love
Go
Other circumstances
Where your life
Is not threatened
And it feels like love
Stick around
It could well be love
I think a lot of people

Get married
In a formal setting
Of getting married
Wedding dress
Church
That's not where
The marriage starts
The marriage
Should start
Way before that
But a lot of people
Call that the marrying
The marriage
Someone said to me once
They believe in marriage
Because it's your
Announcement
Making it public
An announcement
To everybody
On the day
That's what the ceremony is
You're announcing
To everybody
That this is
The commitment you've made

And because you've
Made that commitment
To everybody
Now you have to keep it
Because you've made it public
You've made a show
This is what I'm going to do
This is my vow
And I'm going to do this
And you have to hold me
Accountable
Because I've told you all now
So I've got to do this
Because I told them
That I'm getting married
Until death do us part
I'm going to stay
With this person
And they told me
That's why they think
The marriage is important
And I get that
And there could be
Something to that
But I really don't believe
That's where it starts

I think it's about
The marriage
The marrying
Or the reason why
You step
Into that ceremony
And have the wedding
I believe
It should start
Way before that
The marriage
The marrying
Of those people
I think that
Should be the end thing
Marriage should happen
Before the ceremony
The becoming one
I believe it should happen
Way before you tell
Anybody anything
Otherwise
It's just a show
And it's not
Going to last long
I think I've seen enough

Broken marriages
And stories I've heard
Of broken marriages
That far outweigh
The successful marriages
Enough to make me
Never want to get married
I always hold the thought that
I will meet someone
That I feel
Will make me feel
That none of that matters
That makes me
Forget all of that
That I've seen
And I get married
I can definitely say
I've seen more
And close to me too
I don't mean stories
Of people I don't even know
I mean
Real-life situations
Around me
It's enough
To make a person

Not want to ever
Consider getting married
And I'm sure
I'm obviously not
The only one
You have more
Of a positive outlook
But somebody
Who hasn't seen
Anyone in their family
Married
For that length of time
Fifty-six years
Someone who doesn't
Have that representation
Around them
Who hasn't seen that
Is not going to have
The same outlook
On marriage
As you have
That's interesting.

ON TINDER

I've tried Tinder
That's been
My only experience
Of online dating at all
That was my
First introduction
Into any type of
Online dating
If you like
It was Tinder
I mean
It was cool
In terms of
Connecting you
With people
It was easy
You know
It's like an app
In your hand
You have access
To meet people
Swiping
And then
You get to chat

Message
And arrange to meet
That kind of stuff
So it was great
In terms of that
Because I've never
Experienced
Anything
Like it before
In that way
I did go on a few dates
I did indeed
But I also found
One Christmas
This is
Years ago now
That I lost
Two weeks
Of my life
And I don't know
Where it went
Up to now
Two weeks of my life
Just Tindering
Messaging
Back and forth

And stuff
And I know
It was all
Down to Tinder
And I'll never
Get that time back
So yeah
It's good and it's bad.

PATIENCE OVERALL

The big one I learned
Is the one
That I will share
It's patience
Patience
Is so important
First and foremost
Top of the list
Patience
Lack of
Can ruin a lot
Of opportunities
Can stop a lot
Of progress
Can hinder you
Other side notes
To that
Don't be afraid
To do things
On your own
Don't think
That you're only
One person
That you're limited

And cannot
Make things happen
A lot of individual people
On their own
Have made a lot
Of things
Happen
If we look at history
A lot of single people
Without a team
Have made things happen
Then teams
Wanted to get involved
When they saw
That this
One person
Was able to
Do this thing
Not everybody had a team
To start with
So don't be afraid
To do things
On your own
Is another side thing
To that
But overall

Patience
Patience
Patience
Patience
Sometimes
We are like me
As I was
I should say
Early in the process
Wasn't patient
At the time
I had a vision
That no one else
Really saw
At the time
Or very few
People saw
Or at least
The circles I was in
Didn't see
And because of that
I started to question
My vision
And all it was
Is that
I was early

In the process
And didn't
Have the patience
To see it through
And just keep going
And it hindered me
And it's only after
Experiencing that
That I learned
What had happened
And having to reset
So my advice
Would be
Patience
Overall
Patience
Is so important
And it can
Add a lot to you
When you're patient
You think it's
Taking away
We often think
Patience
Is taking away
From us

Waiting
But often
It's adding
And that's something
I wish
I knew
As a youngster.

PRESERVATION OF THE PRICELESS

Writing
Making films
Video blogging
Just ideas
And things
That I've thought about
That I've not really
Heard anyone else
Speak about
Or crazy ideas
That are true to life
But don't
Necessarily exist
That I'd like to
Explore
And open up
People's minds to
I like a lot of the things
I create
I take pleasure
In knowing
That it's going to
Stimulate conversation
Or in the very least

If not external
Open conversation
With other people
That it's going to create
Internal dialogue
For people
They'll see or hear it
And they'll go away
And think about things
In a different way
From the way
They were thinking about them
And I love that whole thing
And also
It kind of
Gives a little opening
To my mind as well
How I think
And my thoughts
And little
Pieces of myself
Are being shared
I got very strongly
Into vlogging
A lot because
I realise

There's two things
That are happening
It's something
I did before
But I kind of left off
Like ten years ago
And I kind of got back into it
Got passionate about it again
There's two things
That are happening
In creating videos and stuff
I get to satisfy
My creative need
Desire
Lust
Whatever you
Want to call it
And I also look at
How much I would
Love to go back now
And be able to
Go online for example
And pull up a video of my
Great-great great-great-great
Grandparents
And watch them

Doing something
No matter how random
Watch them sitting
At a table eating food
Or watch them
Getting ready
On their way to work
Watch them
With their children
Or parents
Taking them to school even
Or just sitting talking
About how
Disgusting this drink is
Or whatever
Just the joy that would be
How precious
And priceless
That would be
For me to be able
To go online and do that
Of course I can't
Because that material
Doesn't exist
The second thing is
As I was saying

About what's satisfying
And gratifying for me
Is the fact that
I know I'm creating
That same thing
For my descendants
So they will have something
To pull up
And look at
And reference
Where they came from
Their lineage
Their ancestors
Their great-great-great-great
Grandparents
Or granddad
It's like preservation
For those
Who will come after
And satisfying my own
Creative desires
In the present
And sharing
I learn a lot
About myself
When I make a vlog

94

Or video
Or whatever
I learn a lot about myself
Sometimes I just
Put the camera on
And just let it go
And just speak
Because I never know
What I'm going to
Speak about that day
Sometimes I have a topic
In mind
Sometimes I don't
I'll just speak
And I learn a lot
About myself
And I know in turn
Other people
Will learn something
And on it goes
There's a lot of things
Happening
One of the things
I've learned
Is that I can just
Do what I just said

Putting the camera on
And just going
Just talking
And seeing what comes
And things that are
In my mind
I didn't know
Were there
Or you forgot
That you'd learned
Or experienced
Or encountered
What I've really learned
Is that nothing
Is lost
Nothing is gone
Any experience
That you have
You think it's
A far distant thing
And that's definitely
One of the things
I've learned
That nothing is lost
Everything is there.

RISE OF THE ROBOTS

Okay
Is that her first one
Ah her first phone
Wow
I was much older
When I got my first phone
How old is she
Ten
I don't even know
If I knew
What a phone was
At ten
Apart from
The rotary one
You had to
Stick your finger in
And wind it round
To get the numbers
I'll tell you why
Kids having phones
These days
So parents
Can contact them
Coming home

Is a bit BS to me
This whole thing
Of having a phone
Knowing where they are
And being able
To contact them
If anything happens
That kind of thing
Because we didn't have it
Growing up
We didn't have it
And we survived
Our generation
Did not have
Mobile phones
So we had to
Find our way home
And we got there
Because
We're still here right
So we got there safely
And back again
The argument could be
Times have changed
And things are
Worse now

For a young adult
Walking home
From school
Kind of thing
That could be
The argument
I don't know
If that's true
If they're any worse
Than they were
Back in the day
I think
It's a little bit BS
Because we didn't have it
We didn't have that
You're more likely
As a kid
To get beat up
For your phone now
Or get kidnapped
Or mugged
Or something happen
To you
For your phone
That you're carrying
More than actually

Anything else
That would've happened
To you before
Or without it
That's quite interesting
I guess it's all time
And it's all convenience
Everything is convenience
Everything that you look at
That's presented
Is about saving time
Everything
Saving time
And convenience
And obviously
Contact
Being able to
Contact someone immediately
Is obviously one of those
Time-saving things
Anything other than that
Is just like
Peace of mind isn't it
You know
Peace of mind
Like how they say

Get insurance
For your phone
Extra whatever amount
Of money a month
For peace of mind
And again
It's a saving time thing
Because
That's so that if
You lose your phone
You know
That you can get one
Straight away again
It's all about time saving
I guess it's peace of mind
For the parents
Waiting in the wild
And in the wilderness
It might be good
For her to have it
Anything could happen
Yes, understood
My question is
Back in the day
What did we do
It's interesting

How we've changed
How we act
Because we
Have this device
I'm thinking
What would I have done
Back in the day
I'm supposed to
Be somewhere
At a certain time
It's interesting
Just observing that
I would have waited
I would have just waited
I was supposed to wait
At a certain place
At a certain time
I would just wait
I would have just
Waited I guess
Any numbers
That have
Introduced themselves
Since the introduction
Of your mobile
You don't rely on your brain

To remember them
They're all stored
In your phone
With my mum's number
The other day
I had to write it down
On something
And I couldn't remember it
I had to go check
And I hate that
Because I know that number
So well
And she's had it
All the time
For years
It just goes to show
What's happening to us
It's likc I mentioned before
It's not long
The robots
Are coming to kill us
And we don't realise it
They're killing us
I should say
It's happening
They're taking over

The phone is a robot
The phone is an android
It's already happening
It's taking over
We have it in our hands
The thing that's going to kill us
We're interacting
With parts of it everyday
Parts of the machine
That's going to kill us
And take us down
The phone is smart
We're dumbing down
We're being dumbed down
The whole time
They're Android phones now
That's just literally like a robot
Imagine
You've got this device
That's called an iPhone
Another reason
Why the iPhone thing
Is interesting
Is because it's very personal
Like 'I'
You know

104

It's like 'Me'
It's very antisocial
It's like taking away
The human side of us
Where we interact
With people
And sit down in groups
And talk
The iPhone
And the iPad
It's all like...
You know
Isolation
It's interesting
It's interesting where it's all going.

SELF REFLECTIONS

A lot of the time
People don't like what they see
They don't like that reflection
They don't like
What you represent for them
Nothing wrong with you
What offends them
Is the fact that who you are
Shows them who they're not
Who they feel they should be
But they're not
It's an interesting one
Reflection
Mirror
Representation
It's you shining your light
Without even knowing
On them
And them being able
To see themselves
Seeing what they want
What they're not
What they want to be
What they wish they could be

106

They don't hate you
They don't dislike you
And if they do
If we can say that
It's not because of anything
You've done that is wrong
It's to do with
What you show them to be
To themselves
Like a mirror
Like a reflection
They see you
They see themselves
They're either like you
Or they're not
And they either like that fact
Or they don't
So don't worry about you
You're fine
You're doing just fine
Do you
Keep doing you
As you've been doing you
And don't worry about haters
Don't worry about dislikers
Don't worry about people

Dissing your ambitions
And trying to put you down
And belittle you
And all of that stuff
You know it
Because you've experienced it
You may be experiencing it
Right now
But I tell you
From my experience
It's not that they
Don't like you
It's nothing you're doing wrong
You keep doing what you're doing
It's something
That they have to deal with
You're a representation
Of what they wish they could be
Perhaps you show them
What they're not
And they don't have
An easy time with it
So every time
You come around
You're an offence to them
You're offensive

And it's a lot to do with that
Don't take that to heart at all
Just keep doing you
Hopefully they'll come around
And realise that they can do
Just as you're doing
Be just as you are
Or better
For themselves
It's not you
It's nothing to do with you
It's nothing you need to change
Or any way you need to be
Don't take it on board
You can't
You just can't afford to
People need to
Deal with themselves
Basically
Keep shining your light
And being who you are
Just do that
Just keep being who you are
It's not about you
It's not that they don't like you
It's not you at all

It's them
If they were in a different place
Within themselves
They would love you
So it's not about you
Just as you are
They would love you
It's not about you
They dislike the reflection
That you cast
And it's not your fault
You're just being yourself
You show them
Where they're lacking
Where they're not whole
You show them
The inadequacies
Within themselves
Just by being you
And shining your light
And being a reflection
Of the world
It's not about you
It's none of your business
What people
Who are not happy

With themselves
Are doing
Or saying
Negatively against you
It is of no benefit to you
It's none of your business
It is of no value to you
It doesn't progress you
In any way
So don't focus on it
Just keep doing you
It's nothing
That you need to
Worry about
That you need to change
It's something
That they need to deal with
And hopefully
They will in time
So that they can progress
So that they can advance
To where they're in a place
That doesn't
Make them feel a way
Whenever they see you
When they see you

Progressing
None of your business
None of your regard
Nothing for you to
Worry about
Just keep doing you
Keep shining
And keep growing
Keep moving forward
Keep putting one foot
In front of the other
In the right direction
And when you see
You're making progress
And people
Are not liking it
Keep going.

SOCIALLY AWKWARD

They don't really count
Because they know you
If that makes sense
And you're likely
To be more
Comfortable
Around those people
So they wouldn't necessarily
See you
As socially awkward
Because you kind of
Broke that thing
That makes you
Socially awkward
People that you're used to
Being around
That wall or that shell
That you're inside
As a socially awkward person
Is gone
It falls away
When you're used to
Being around people
That you're used to

When you're not
Around strangers
I think it helps
Your best friend
Won't see you
As socially awkward
Or maybe they would
Maybe they know you best
Maybe they know
You're socially awkward
Maybe they like you for it
You know
I like socially awkward people
Like myself
I understand them
I think that's what it is
I understand them
I think I have some kind of
Empathy for them
Because I know what is
To be that way
The right friends get it
They get that you
Need that space
Sometimes I think
That parents

Understand it less
Than maybe like a friend
Parents are funny
I mean
Not every parent
But a lot of parents
Don't get their own children
Why they are
The way they are
Why they
Behave in certain ways
It's outside sources
Or forces
That if they do
Come to understand
They come to
The understanding
Through outside elements
They may begin to understand
Their own child
Through their child's friend
Or through their child's peers
You know
Teachers
Whatever might teach them
Things about their child

They may not even
Be aware of
Why their child is like that
Or they may not even
Notice it
They may think
My child is just weird
Why are you not like
The other children
I don't know
But for me
I just I feel like
I'm a socially
Awkward person
It's only as a performer
And not having to
Be in certain circumstances
That makes me
Appear not that way
To the average person
I'm okay in crowds
I'm okay greeting
And meeting people
And being in environments
Where there is strangers
And crowds around

People I don't know
My natural state
Is just to be to myself
And in my shell
And reclusive
I'm can very much
Stay away to myself
For a long time indoors
And not see anyone
And be quite happy
I think I was
Forced into situations
That didn't allow me
To stay in my shell
As a child
I was put in situations
Like going out
To social gatherings
And stuff
Having to interact
Be it church
Be it school
Later life
Performing obviously
You have to
Come out of that shell

If you're going to
Present yourself
On stage to an audience
It's the same thing
With modelling
Again it's an audience
Catwalk
You had to put away
That part of yourself
And summon
This other part of yourself
That appeared to be the opposite
To a socially awkward person
I grew up an only child
For a period as well
I think that can
Help you remain
Socially awkward
But maybe
I have the wrong term for it
Maybe I'm not
A socially awkward person
At all
Or maybe
I'm just different
And weird

Maybe we
Label ourselves too much
Maybe we just are
What we are
Well we are what we are
At the end of the day
People just
Put labels on it
What I do love
Is that we're all
Not the same
We're individual
We have our own
Little things
That make us individual
And weird and strange
The weird and strange
Is not bad
I like the weird
And strange
It gives variation
And spice to life
Imagine if
Everything was the same
We had the same soup
Every day

Tasted the same
Looked the same
Smelled the same
Spice of life
We need different things
Different experiences
Different tastes
A lot of people
Don't like change
I'm like that too
I love change
Obviously
Like you know
For example
Going to different places
Meeting different people
I do like that
Experiencing
Different things
We can do
You know
Get a new outfit
I mean
I like change
And I like new things
But there's things

I like to stay the same
You know
Like most people
When you have to
Learn something new
Like a new software
When you were using
A particular type
Of software
For such a long period
You don't really want to
Learn a new one
All over again
You kind of
Like the way things are.

STEAMY SEX SCENE

Received a message
On my messenger
It's just a little weird
A little strange
I have to question
I don't know
Are people sane
Okay
Do you ever get
The weirdest messages
Craziest messages
Strange message I received
Eight o'clock this morning
I will share it with you
For the purpose of this
We shall call this person
By another name
We shall call them Mary
Okay, so here we go
Strange message...

Mary:
Hi Phoenix
I want to do a steamy sex scene with you
Is that possible
I have my own business
And production company
On safe sex
Got a budgie
It's pregnant
I raise them
That's also my business

Me:
Hi Mary
Of course
Everything's possible
Tell me more

Mary:
Lol what's your number
Got my business

Then Mary posts a picture
Of a green coach van...

Me:
Congratulations

Mary:
Thank you
So you're not interested
Get paid fifty pounds an hour lol
I'm going to church now
Going to church
Jesus is Christ

Me:
Yes
Super interested
Added a smiley face emoji

Mary:
Okay

Me:
Have a good day at church

Mary:
Need your number lol

Okay will ask Idris Elba

124

I know where he's filming
In North London

Me:
Best to get me by email

Mary:
There's a long waiting list
To be on my books
And waiting time of six years
Take care
Wish you best of luck
Got someone else
Bye

Me:
Thanks
For the entertainment
This morning

Mary:
Okay lol
I'm being serious lol
Working with actor
From Footballers Wives
Bye lol

I don't know
I've written it as it was
My responses
Were based on the fact that
I kind of got that this wasn't real
This couldn't possibly be serious
But I was willing to see if it was
So you know
Email me
Anything's possible
I'm interested
See where it goes, you know
Just give the person
The benefit of the doubt
This can't be serious
What do you all make of it
What do you make
Of this message
And also
What's the weirdest
Craziest message
You've received recently?

TEACHER ATTRACTION

I always feel like
I just attract teachers
Teachers are just
Attracted to me
I don't know what it is
I always seem
To attract teachers
I don't know
Do I somehow
Seem teachable
An easy to train
And teach
To adapt to new ways
Kind of guy maybe
I don't know
Student
I don't know
It just happens
I've noticed it
And I don't know why
It's always teacher types
Teachers of some field
Some form of
Teaching job

Or role
Or career
But it involves teaching
I always seem
To attract teachers
Do I seem dumb
In need of some teaching
Some schooling
Some guidance
I don't know
Or is it me
Am I attracted to teachers
Because I'm
Looking for someone
Who can maybe
Teach me a little something
I don't know
Someone with
A little bit of intelligence
Someone who is
Capable
Of sharing knowledge
I don't know
I'm just
Stream of consciousness here
Just analysing here

Pondering here
It's interesting
Maybe I look
Manageable
Easy to teach
I don't know
Maybe I just look
Like a child lost
Needing some
Guidance in life
Maybe it's me
Maybe I'm just
Attracted to teachers
Maybe I'm just
Looking for someone
With a little brain
I mean
Not a little brain
But I mean
A little bit of brains
You know
Someone who can
Show me something
Teach me things
I've never seen before
Never experienced before

Maybe
This is all just processes
You know
It's interesting
What we attract and why
What we're attracted to
And why
It's fascinating
I don't know
There is something here
I haven't got to it yet
But I have noticed it
Why do we attract
What we attract
Why is
What is attracted to us
Attracted to us
Why
I'm supremely
Fascinated by this
I've noticed in the past
And not so distant past either
Teachers from all fields
All different fields
And forms of teaching
They just seem

To be attracted to me
And me attracted to them
I don't know why
I don't know what's going on
I don't know what's in the plan
I don't know who's playing this game
Moving us around
Like chess pieces
Forcing us together
I don't know
What the gods
Are doing up there
I don't know what's happening
I don't know
I don't know
I don't know
But I know
That I always seem
To connect
With teachers
I don't know if it's me
Giving off
That I need something
In the way of teaching
And guidance
And schooling

And help
And tutoring
In my life
I don't know
Or if it's me
And I'm just
Attracted to symbols
Of the same
Or just in search
Of somebody
That could possibly
Teach me something in life
Somebody with a brain
Somebody who offers something
Who offers some kind of guidance
I don't know
I don't know
I don't know
I don't know
I don't have any answers
This is not about answers
This is not about the answers
This is about the questions
The whys
And the hows
And the whats

And the whens
I don't know
I'm merely a student
In all of this
Merely a student
Dating
Relationships
Sexual attraction
Do not ask me
I have no idea
I'm learning
I'm learning
I'm learning
I don't know
This is merely
Observational
A lot of my
Previous relationships
Partners
Lovers
Whatever you want to call it
Have been teachers
Teachers
What a privilege
To be called a teacher
Wow

I'm a teacher
That's serious business
I teach people
How amazing
It could be because
I left school at sixteen
And didn't return
To any further education
Whatsoever
Apart from that which
I taught myself
Self-taught as they say
Maybe
I'm lacking something
Maybe
I feel I'm missing
Some form of education
From those teachers
That no longer were
When I went off
Into the world
With without any intention
Of going on
To further education
I had the intention
Actually

I just didn't go that way
By sixteen I had a job
Yes…
Interesting
Who knows
Maybe
Just maybe
Teachers find themselves
Attracted to me
Because they see
That I can teach them something
Maybe they want to be
In a position
Of receiving knowledge
Of not always
Being the teacher
Sometimes maybe
They just want to be
The student
And they see
That I am someone
Who can offer something
In that department
Someone with a brain
Who can expand them
Mentally

Someone they can learn from
We just don't know
It's all merely
My stream of consciousness
Observational
We may never have the answer
Maybe I'm a teacher
In some way
Maybe it's teacher
Attracted to teacher
That could be it
I don't label myself
As a teacher
But maybe there's
Some teaching in there
Maybe I'm
Teaching people something
In some way
Or have done
Or will do
I don't know
Maybe that's it
Maybe there's a teacher gene
That we're both
Attracted to
In each other

I don't know
Interesting
Tell me what types
You usually attract
Or are attracted to.

THE KILL OF CHASING

Traveling
Did so much for me
It just gave me
So much time
To think
About the direction
I was going in
With my stuff
And what I was doing
And where I really
Should have been going
Looking at the vehicle
More so than
Where I want to get to
My destination
And it gave me a chance
To really realise
I'm looking at the vehicle
And not the destination
I found what it was about
For me again
It was about the creativity
And the work
Doing that

Not chasing auditions
I hate auditions
I can act
I mean, I enjoy it
I love it
I love the fun of it
But not the process
That's put in place
That everyone follows
My process as a poet
Is very different
In terms of learning lines
And having time to work
With the material
If you haven't
Been to drama school
And trained that way
It's a very different process
You may be able to
Act very well
But there's a process
I'm used to having more time
With material
And spending time with it
You don't always get that
With auditions

I find that process
Quite stressful
And the waiting
I find as an actor
You're a waiter
More than anything else
You're more of a waiter
Than an actor
You're waiting
For your agent to call
You're waiting
To find out
If you've got the casting
Or the call back
Or you're waiting
For the next casting
And then
You go to the casting
You're waiting
To be seen
You're waiting
To find out
If you've got the part
Then you're waiting
For a decision
Then you're waiting

Waiting for dates
Waiting for the next one
Then when you get on set
If you get the part
You're waiting
To do your part
Then you're waiting
For the film to come out
Then you're waiting
To see if you're in it
Or not
And then
You may be in it
You may not be
That may go well
That may not
And then you're waiting
For the next casting
The next audition
Then it goes around
And around and around
So you spend
A lot of time waiting
Waiting for your agent
To call
When you're at home

There's only so many
Books you can read
There's only so many
TV shows you can watch
When you really want to be
Doing your craft
You really want to be
Creating
And that's the frustration
That's the part that inspired me
To start making my own stuff
And finishing
I enjoy the creative process
I'm not aspiring to be
Mr Hollywood actor
That's not me
I know people
Who are doing that
And that's fine
But the year I took touring
Seeing other countries
And other cultures
And traveling
Really gave me time to think
About where I'm at
And where I want to be

And what direction
I want to go
With what I want to do
And it really
Brought me back to myself
Not that I got away
Well I got away a little bit
I think
And it really gave me
A chance to think
I'm not that guy
Chasing like that
But I love acting
I love the process
I'm a creative
I love creating
It's what I've always done
And acting
Allows me do that
And that's what I love
I got into the machine of it
A bit too much
And it's not for me
If something I do
Turns out
To go that direction

Then fine
But I'm not chasing that
I just want to do good work
I love creating
I love the art
I love cinematography
And film
And photography
That whole process I love
That's why I used to
Love being a film extra
On set
Watching
And observing
I'm really passionate
About that stuff
I'm getting back into it
Basically
I'm really excited
About producing
When I say producing
I mean creating
And putting out content
Be it in video blog form
You know
Me talking to camera

Or talking about my day
Or in a film
For film scenes
That I've created
I didn't fully appreciate
Any of that
And I realised
How important that is now
And I wish I'd kept up doing it
And I'm trying to document
As much of me as I can
And sharing that
Long story short
I'm really excited
That I'm
Producing things
And editing them now
And just
Getting them out
Getting stuff out.

TRUTH IS OUT THERE

I don't believe
We're the only
Life force
In existence
On all these
Different planets
I don't believe
We're the only life
In existence here on earth
I definitely believe
They've been with us
I believe we're not alone
They walk among us
I really do
I believe in all that stuff
I used to watch The X-Files
And all that stuff
I'm into all that
I believe we're not alone
The meaning of life
I've got to come up with
Something cool for that
Like something just plain
And that's the meaning of life

But I haven't got it yet
I'm still learning it to be fair
I don't think anyone knows
I think there's a lot of
Philosophical answers
About the meaning of life
But I don't think
Anyone really knows
I think you get here
And you have to
Kind of find out
You don't really know
You don't come knowing
You're figuring it out
Your whole life
Like what's the meaning
You might discover a meaning
Or come up with a meaning
But is that really what it means
I toy with this one a lot
About the afterlife
And whether we're just dead
I like to believe there's more
I like to believe we go on
I like to believe
I'll see my grandmothers again

I like to believe
They're watching over me
I'll meet those people again
In spirit form
Or is that whole thing
Of thinking that there's more
Beyond this life
A kind of thing
We've given ourselves
To feel better about dying
More comfortable about dying
We've just created this thing of
There's more after it
Just so we feel better
About the end
I don't know
I think...
I definitely think there's more
Than meets the eye
I definitely think
There's more than
What exists
On this plane that we see
This earth plane
I believe
There's existence of life

Outside of that
Maybe life
Might not be the right word
But other energies
Other forces
Other things going on
Well there definitely is
We know that
There's all that stuff
Going on
Outside of the earth
That's proven
Science
Do I think
There will ever be
Peace on earth?
I think there is a possibility
For peace
I think the possibility is there
Whether or not there will be
We obviously don't know
But I definitely
Believe
That the possibility is there
I think the positive side
Of human nature

Is within all of us
So I believe that the potential
Is definitely there
For people to live
In peace
Everything else
Has been learned behaviour
Like sharing
And caring
And loving
I believe we could live like that
A World War III?
I believe there's a possibility
For that too
The possibility
Is definitely there
I mean
Look how long
Nations have been at war
What started those ones
Another one could develop
And be a World War III
It could happen
I hope it doesn't
I'd love there to be
Peace on earth

But it could definitely happen
There's been one
There's been two
Nothing to stop a third
Everything that was in place
For the first one to start
It still exists
Firstly
Human beings
The second one
Same thing
Third one
It could happen
It's the same people
The same human beings
With the same things
That cause wars
Within them
It's not the machines
And the bombs
And all that stuff
They don't create themselves
And move themselves
Man has to do all that stuff
Man has to send out
Those armies

And those
Destructive weapons
For nothing
Politics
And power
And money
And possession
That's what it is
And greed
And that still exists
One hundred percent
I definitely believe
There could be another one
I don't want to see one
That's another thing
You made me think about
When you asked me
That question
I feel that it could counteract
What I've already said
Or contradict
But I will say it
I feel that
How the world has advanced
Since those world wars
And technology

And all of that
Just the way
The world has progressed
I feel that
It wouldn't necessarily
Need to be with bombs
And millions of people dying
I feel that there's
A different type of war
One that you might not
Even be aware you're in
World War III
Could be happening now
But just in a different way
People not getting blown up
And killed
It could be psychological
In the way that
The world is run
Who's in control
Who's in power
Why they're in power
What they're doing
While they're in power
What changes they make
That everyone else has to follow

The governments I mean
And so on
And so forth
It doesn't necessarily
Have to be
Sending out planes
To bomb people
A cure for cancer?
I believe it exists already
I believe the cure
For a lot of things
Including cancer
Exists
I think it's been
Around so long
I'm sure that a cure for it
Has been developed by now
I think cancer
Is a thing that can be cured
And I think it's also a thing
That's used
For population control
It's my crazy mind
I believe
It's like a lot of things
About money

I believe the cure
For a lot of things
Is out there
But I believe
If they were distributed
To cure the people
That need them
People wouldn't be
Dependent on
Pharmaceuticals
And hospitals
And doctors
And a lot of those people
Would be out of a job
And I feel
That's why
We don't know about them
That's why we don't have
Access to them
These cures
This is why
You go to your doctor
And you go to the hospital
And that system
Needs to keep running
Because if everyone was cured

And didn't need
To go to the hospital
That's a lot of people
Out of a job
In those industries
No one would
Need those tablets
And those placebos
I believe that
You know
It's all a system
It's in place to keep people
In the positions they're in
War
Same thing
It's to keep people
In the positions
That they're in
And attain greater
Greed
Is an important word
In all of it
Do I believe there's aliens?
I definitely believe
There's aliens
And they walk among us

Don't you think
They would be more
Advanced than us
Or do you feel
They're not as
Advanced as us
But they're aliens
Can you imagine that
Imagine
We're more advanced
Than them
I like to think
They're more advanced
And they're watching
Everything
And they intervene
When they feel they need to
Or maybe
They're planning to come back
Maybe they're the Jesus
That's to come back
Maybe they're the rapture
And all that stuff in the Bible
And you know
Ezekiel's wheels
And all that

If you read that stuff
Then it just goes
Into a whole thing
Do you think
They watch our movies
Do you think
An alien saw me
As a First Order Stormtrooper
That's class
If you look at it
Talking about Star Wars
Those are aliens
They don't live on earth do they
To us they're aliens
Darth Vader
All of them
You know
Traversing the galaxy
At light speed
They're aliens
They don't live here.

WAY OF THE WORLD

I think we're just
Reaching a place
Where change
Has to happen
It's not that time
Where it would have
Never ever happened
You know
Where things
Were structured
In such a way
That there was no way
That was going to happen
It was just a different time
I feel now
The times are changing
In a way
Where those structures
Are falling away
And that change
Is going to happen
Because of the way
The world is
You know

You just can't
Hold back things
The natural way
We're all here on the planet
We're not all one race
We're different
We're different cultures
We're black
We're white
We're different colours
All that kind of stuff
And that's just
The way of the world
And there's only so much
You can hold back
The way of the world
Before it breaks
We can only
Hold back a tsunami
Or try to
For so long
Until it says that's it
I'm coming
We can't change what is
We can alter things
And hold things back

But when it's ready
The world decides
And the same
With the fact that
We're all different
And we all have a right
To be in every single place
That's available to be in
Eventually
We're going to get there
If we have the desire
To get there
We're not
Getting in that place
This group of people said
We can't be there
We can't have that
It's only a matter of time
Before we get there
Because it's
The way of the world
No one controlled
Us coming here
In different colours
And shapes
And forms

And sizes
No one said let's create that
No one human said
Okay
We're not going to have this
We're going to have that
We're going to have this
In regards to human beings
So it's just like everything else
The trees
There's going to be trees
Forget trees for a minute
There's going to be
World disasters
Like natural disasters
They're going to happen
Because
It's the way of the world
It's the way of the earth
It's the way of the planet
Just like we came
From the earth
It's the way of the earth
We have to exist
We have to coexist
So for a group of people

162

Who don't like that
Who want to change that
To change
The way of the world
Change the natural form
And progression of things
It's only for so long
They're going to
Be able to do that
And the time now
Is changing
Where they're losing
That footing
Of trying to control that
So you're going to see
More inclusion
You're going to see change
You're going to see black
Marrying white
White marrying black
You know
In the royal family
And so on
Right across the board
In everything
And I know we were talking

About Meghan and stuff
But in everything
You're going to see more of it
Because that structure
That has been put in place
Where people want to control
Who has what
And who is entitled to what
It's falling away
So you're going to see more
More of that
You can only stop
That natural thing
For so long
We all came here one way
You can't say
Stop one group of people
Because we're all entitled
That's the problem
For some
They don't want others
To have that entitlement
But the problem is
We're all here on the planet
We're all entitled
That's it

No one is better
Than anyone else
So because of that
There's only so long
Someone's going to be able
To prevent someone else
From gaining
What they're
Supposed to gain
And getting
What they're supposed to get
And receiving
What they're entitled to
People want to take
Everything
For themselves
And separate this group
They're not worthy
We're going to
Keep them down
And we're going to rise up
That's turning
On its head now
And things like
You know
The royal wedding

Things like Trump
And Barack Obama
Entering office
And films like Black Panther
Breaking the box office
These all show me
That change is happening
It's just happening
There's only so long
We can prevent
Those kind of things
Because those are all
New things
Why haven't they
Happened before
And that's because
Things are changing
Maybe not as swift
As some of us would like
But there's changes
Coming about
And you can't stop
What's right
Only for so long
Because it's not
The natural order

166

Something breaks down
Either you
Subconsciously know
You're doing wrong
And it crumbles
Or the natural order
Just takes over
Law of attraction
All that kind of stuff
The universe just speaks
And says no more
It's going to happen
It's just going to happen
In its own time
It's going to
Take care of itself
The earth is just like that
It takes care of itself
If you really look at it
It does what it needs to do
Humans don't
Stand in the way of that
It keeps going.

WHAT I LIKE IN BED

Nobody don't want no
Bag of bones in the bed
Nobody don't want to
Rub up against bones all night
It's not realistic
People trying to get surgery
To look like that
And it's just not real
Trying to look like
Barbie dolls
It's just not real
Taking out ribs
All that kind of stuff
It's just not realistic
You look at those
Ancient figures
They used to carve
Whether you go back
To the Egyptians
Or the Greeks
Or whatever
You find
They were fuller figured
Fuller figured women

168

Look at any of them
Those ancient
African figures
They carved out
That's what they worshipped
That's what they looked up to
That's what they found beautiful
That was their symbol of beauty
Women with full figures
Big hips
Big ass
Big breasts
Everything
You look back at that
You'll see
I don't know where
This idea came from
These stick figure women
That are supposed to be
The symbol of beauty
I just don't subscribe to it
It's not attractive to me
I mean
I find all women attractive
But I know
That I definitely appreciate

A fuller figured woman
Hands down
That's definitely
What I want to be in a bed with
When it comes to snuggling up
And being cuddled
And snugly
And all the rest of stuff
That comes with cuddling
And snuggling
I want to feel something
I want to feel some energy
Some warmth
And some size
It's just more of it
It's just like cuddly
There's more of it
I've got a long time
To be in the company of bones
So while I'm alive
Give me some flesh
Give me some meat
Give me something to squeeze
And hold onto
That's real.

YOU ARE ENOUGH

It's early
In the morning
Three o'clock
One should be
Sleeping
But one is not
One is filled
With much
Energy
And love
One wants to
Hug
The whole world
And tell them
They're enough
You
Are enough.

ABOUT THE AUTHOR

Phoenix James is an award winning Writer, Poet, Author and Spoken Word Recording Artist. He began performing his poetic words live on stages across the UK in 1998. His debut spoken word poetry album, *The A.R.T.I.S.T,* was released in 2000. His first limited edition printed collection of poetry, *To Whom It May Concern,* was published in 2003. He has toured and performed his poetry internationally since 2004. He has appeared in films, on television and radio shows, and collaborated with other artists, singer-songwriters, actors, musicians, filmmakers and producers. In 2013, he wrote, directed and produced the feature length mock documentary film, *Love Freely but Pay for Sex.* Phoenix James has written, recorded and released several spoken word poetry albums including, *Phenzwaan Now & Forever* (2009), *A Patchwork Remedy for A Broken Melody* (2020), *FREE* (2021), *Haven for the Tormented* (2021), *With All That Said* (2022), and *Remixes* Volumes: 1 & 2 (2022).

If you enjoyed reading this book, please leave a review online. The author reads every review and they help new readers discover his work.

PHOENIX JAMES

Photo by Phoenix James

Phoenix James lives in London, England.

Connect with Phoenix James on his online social media platforms via www.linktr.ee/ Phoenix_James and say you've read this book. To contact or learn more about Phoenix James and his creative journey or to receive updates via his Newsletter Mailing List, visit his official website at www.PhoenixJamesOfficial.com

Phoenix James Official

www.ingramcontent.com/pod-product-compliance
Lightning Source LLC
Chambersburg PA
CBHW021231090426
42740CB00006B/486